Spiritual Messages from
the Guardian Spirit of

Ayatollah Khamenei

and

General

Soleimani

FOR THE MUTUAL UNDERSTANDING BETWEEN IRAN AND THE U.S.

RYUHO OKAWA

HS PRESS

Copyright © 2020 by Ryuho Okawa
Original title: *America niwa Mienai Iran no Honshin*
- Khamenei shi Shugorei Soleimani Shireikan no Reigen -
HS Press is an imprint of IRH Press Co., Ltd.
Tokyo
ISBN 13: 979-888737-011-8
Cover Image: Bart Sadowski/Azat1976/shutterstock.com
First Edition (updated)

Contents

1

Spiritual Messages from Major General Soleimani

2

Spiritual Messages from The Guardian Spirit of Ayatollah Khamenei

Preface

It's an astonishing reality. Just after the New Year, at about 1:20 AM, U.S. forces killed Major General Soleimani, the commander directly under the supreme leader of Iran, by drone attack while he was riding in a car in Iraq. His spirit visited me in Tokyo when I was just going to bed, only a day after his death, while his remains were being transferred from Iraq to Tehran, Iran. On the next day, January 5, I talked about it in my lecture, "The Lecture on *The Laws of Steel*," which was broadcasted live all over Japan. Iran mourned his death for three days, and as his coffin was being buried, launched a dozen of short-range ballistic missiles to the U.S. bases at the same hour and minute as when he was killed.

The attack came about 24 hours after the guardian spirit of Iran's Ayatollah Khamenei visited me late at night and predicted it. His spiritual message is recorded as Chapter 2.

Major General Soleimani and Ayatollah Khamenei have undying faith and unwavering heart. I felt so, and at the same time, I was running tears.

U.S. President Trump might have been thinking that, if he assassinated the boss of terrorists, he will be welcomed as a liberator by the people of Iran and Iraq.

Sincerely, I ask both countries in confrontation to understand each other better, while cherishing faith which is the lifeline that ties Iran and Japan.

With this urgent publication, I hope you can learn the true intention of Iran that the U.S. cannot see and that most Japanese people cannot understand. There needs understanding, not a quagmire of war.

Ryuho Okawa
Master & CEO of Happy Science Group
Jan. 10, 2020

1

Spiritual Messages from
Major General Soleimani

Originally recorded in Japanese, on January 4, 2020
at Special Lecture Hall, Happy Science, Japan
and later translated into English

Qasem Soleimani (1957 - 2020)

An Iranian major general who was born in Rabor County, Kerman Province, Iran. Joined the Iran Revolutionary Guard Corps (IRGC) in 1979. Soleimani served well in the Iran-Iraq War in the 1980s, and became the commander of the 41st Tharallah Division at the age of 30. He was further appointed the commander of Quds Force, a special unit of the IRGC, and commanded Iran's military operations in Iraq and Syria. Soleimani is a national hero in Iran, and Ayatollah Khamenei has called him a "living martyr." In January 2020, U.S. forces attacked and killed him in a drone strike.

Interviewer from Happy Science[*]

Shio Okawa
Aide to Master & CEO

The opinions of the spirit do not necessarily reflect those of Happy Science Group. For the mechanism behind spiritual messages, see end section.

---

[*] Her professional title represents her position at the time of the interview.

1

Iran is Defending Itself

The Iranian commander's spirit pays a visit After the U.S. airstrike

[*Playing in the background is a recording of the author singing lyrics he composed for a new song titled, "Wanderer," inspired by John Lennon's spirit.*]

SHIO OKAWA

You look like you are in pain. [*About 10 seconds of silence.*] Do you like John Lennon? You don't like him? Are you in pain? ... In pain. Why?

MAJOR GENERAL SOLEIMANI

Because I was killed.

SHIO OKAWA

Ohhhhh. Iran's...

MAJOR GENERAL SOLEIMANI

[*Sighs.*] Soleimani.

SHIO OKAWA

Chief of staff... no, captain?

MAJOR GENERAL SOLEIMANI

Commander.

SHIO OKAWA

You were killed, and your body is now on the way to Iran from Baghdad.

MAJOR GENERAL SOLEIMANI

[*Groans.*] My corpse is, yes, but my heart has come here.

SHIO OKAWA

Why?

MAJOR GENERAL SOLEIMANI

I'm sorry for the trouble.

SHIO OKAWA

That's OK. Right now...

MAJOR GENERAL SOLEIMANI

My superiors, the supreme leader and the president...*

SHIO OKAWA

Mr. Khamenei and Mr. Rouhani.

MAJOR GENERAL SOLEIMANI

...have often told me about your people. I have heard from them about you.

---

* Happy Science has recorded spiritual messages from the guardian spirits of Ayatollah Khamenei and President Rouhani several times since June 2019. See Ryuho Okawa, *Nihon no Shimei* (lit. "The Mission of Japan"), *Leader Kokka Nihon no Shinro* (lit. "The Course of Leader Nation Japan"), *Iran no Hanron: Rouhani Daitoryo, Khamenei shi Shugorei, Khomeini shi no Reigen* (lit. "Iran's Counterargument: Spiritual Messages from the Guardian Spirits of President Rouhani and Ayatollah Khamenei, and the Spirit of Ayatollah Khomeini"), and *Igirisu Iran no Tenkanten ni Tsuite* (lit. "On the Turning Point of England and Iran") (all Tokyo: IRH Press, 2019).

"We are fighting a defensive war"
"We are not terrorists"

SHIO OKAWA

According to the U.S., you had plans to kill several hundred American diplomats and others, so they killed you.

MAJOR GENERAL SOLEIMANI

That's a false allegation because it's them who came to invade us. We have not sent our military against them.

SHIO OKAWA

That's true.

MAJOR GENERAL SOLEIMANI

It was them who came to invade us. They established a military base in Saudi Arabia, are allies with Israel, and have been occupying Iraq. And they are after Iran and seeking for an excuse to attack.

SHIO OKAWA

Uh huh.

MAJOR GENERAL SOLEIMANI

It was them who have come to assault us. We are defending.

SHIO OKAWA

Yes.

MAJOR GENERAL SOLEIMANI

We are trying to protect our country. That surely includes guerilla warfare, you know?

SHIO OKAWA

I see.

MAJOR GENERAL SOLEIMANI

We are communicating with and supplying weapons to Shia groups in Iraq who have similar views, so that we can fight together.

SHIO OKAWA

I see. OK.

MAJOR GENERAL SOLEIMANI

But that doesn't make us terrorists. They came to destroy our country, and it's my job as a commander to protect it.

SHIO OKAWA

Defend. Yes.

MAJOR GENERAL SOLEIMANI

It's my job to protect our president and our supreme leader. It's not evil for any country to do this kind of job.

2

Soleimani Analyzes America's Plan

The U.S. wants to make the Middle East One of its states

SHIO OKAWA

I think that the U.S. thinks your country is like North Korea.

MAJOR GENERAL SOLEIMANI

Hmm... But North Korea has been clearly firing actual missiles, one after another.

SHIO OKAWA

Yes, that's true.

MAJOR GENERAL SOLEIMANI

They said they will aim at South Korea, Japan, and other countries, including the U.S. mainland, and have been building missiles. The U.S. calls North Korea "a friend" and does nothing against it, while it calls us "terrorists", doesn't allow us to build missiles and intrudes on us. It bullies you if you are weak, and once you get strong counter offensive weapons, it calls you a friend and reconciles with you. From the Islamic standpoint, it's not justice.

SHIO OKAWA

OK. I think in America, dealing with the Middle East can get more support and votes rather than resolving the crisis in Asia.

MAJOR GENERAL SOLEIMANI

And, that will also draw European interests. I guess so. There is a history. Bush, father and son, made wars two times in Kuwait and Iraq. And, there are people left to still hunt down. They want to actually govern the whole Islamic world, I think.

SHIO OKAWA

I see.

MAJOR GENERAL SOLEIMANI

You know? And, Iran has been the greatest hindrance. Saudi Arabia listens to them (the U.S.), and Iraq also does for the most part, although there are many angry Iraq people now. But there is also Syria who's been in a stalemate and is being pulled by both sides.

SHIO OKAWA

Hmm.

MAJOR GENERAL SOLEIMANI

There is also Jordan who listens, and Turkey who is in a bind due to relationships with Europe and the U.S. The U.S. wants to defang us in order to protect Israel. Everything comes down to that.

SHIO OKAWA

So, it's Mr. Netanyahu.

MAJOR GENERAL SOLEIMANI

I don't know if it's him, but they probably want Israel to act like one of their provinces.

SHIO OKAWA

Ah, I see.

MAJOR GENERAL SOLEIMANI

Like one of their states. "State of the Middle East." We are very disgusted to see the American military base stationed in Saudi Arabia, the land where Islam began and Mecca is located.

It's the U.S. who wants to make a war,
Not Iran

MAJOR GENERAL SOLEIMANI

To have economic trading is fine, but an American military base permanently stationed there means the U.S. has persisting ambition for control over the Middle East. And, that they're looking for the chance to do so.

SHIO OKAWA

I see.

MAJOR GENERAL SOLEIMANI

So, we asked Japan to mediate.

SHIO OKAWA

Uh huh.

MAJOR GENERAL SOLEIMANI

But there was nothing Mr. Abe could do.

There is no way we would ever attack a Japanese oil tanker. So, that was a false accusation set up against us, a plot probably devised by the CIA, and it's so bad. The drone strike on an oil tanker during Mr. Abe's visit, the missile attack, and after all of that, the attack on the Saudi Arabian oil tanker. We don't make such obvious attacks. So, I think they want to make a war.

SHIO OKAWA

The Iranian Revolutionary Guard Corps is seen in the same light as Al-Qaeda, it looks like.

MAJOR GENERAL SOLEIMANI

I think the U.S. has intention to completely destroy our military and defense systems, just as they'd done with Iraq. So, the U.S. is aiming to end the counter-revolution started by Khomeini, the anti-Pahlavi system, during its third leader, and set up a pro-U.S. puppet government.

Judgment on the Iranian Revolution

SHIO OKAWA

After all of that, how should we judge the Iranian Revolution? Was it just a regression toward old traditions?

MAJOR GENERAL SOLEIMANI

It was a kind of restoration to imperial leadership. It was the same as Japan's restoration to imperial rule.

SHIO OKAWA

Oh, so that's why a religious leader is at the top. But on Iran's side...

MAJOR GENERAL SOLEIMANI

Before that, Iran was being Europeanized or Americanized a lot, and with Islamic culture at risk of perishing, we started a counter-revolution. Since pro-American measures were making progress under Pahlavi.

SHIO OKAWA

Westernization, right?

MAJOR GENERAL SOLEIMANI

Yes, yes, yes. If that had continued, all the Iranian traditions and religion would have basically died. They wanted to let our black-robed women wear miniskirts and colorful clothes, and allow them to have sex with many men, have divorces, remarry, drink alcohol, and have fun. That's the kind of country they wanted to create.

SHIO OKAWA

Uh huh.

MAJOR GENERAL SOLEIMANI

I'll acknowledge there are countries that see that as good, so people who seek such things can live in those countries. But that can destroy traditions, sometimes.

SHIO OKAWA

If Iran had a well-functioning economy and no sanctions, the recent protests would have never occurred, you mean?

MAJOR GENERAL SOLEIMANI

Of course. The recent protests were caused by the economic sanctions, for the most part.

SHIO OKAWA

The biggest cause, that's true.

MAJOR GENERAL SOLEIMANI

The target of these protests are about to change though. There is discontent towards the government, but anger against the U.S. is also rising. So, we don't know what the outcome will be right now.

SHIO OKAWA

I see.

The curiosity of
Seeing an Iranian commander's spirit
In Japan soon after his death

SHIO OKAWA

It's been a day since you passed...

MAJOR GENERAL SOLEIMANI

I was killed over there by a drone strike, but I came here, to Tokyo. It's curious.

SHIO OKAWA

Did anyone help you?

MAJOR GENERAL SOLEIMANI

I have a spiritual connection, of course. I'm in the same spiritual line.

SHIO OKAWA

When you were killed, what was it like? You...

MAJOR GENERAL SOLEIMANI

Of course, it was painful.

SHIO OKAWA

It must have been painful, I'm sure.

MAJOR GENERAL SOLEIMANI

It hurt. But being a military man, I was mentally prepared, of course.

"Mr. Trump has bias in his sense of values"

SHIO OKAWA

We are also very sad. We hoped that talks between the U.S. (and Iran)...

MAJOR GENERAL SOLEIMANI

They were quick.

SHIO OKAWA

Too quick.

MAJOR GENERAL SOLEIMANI

It was so quick.

SHIO OKAWA

Because the U.S. elections are coming up...

MAJOR GENERAL SOLEIMANI

The main cause was the demonstration held at the U.S. embassy in Iraq by 4,000 or 5,000 people, mainly Shia people. (The U.S.) wanted to threaten.

SHIO OKAWA

Uh huh. Yes.

MAJOR GENERAL SOLEIMANI

It's not right. They say they are a democracy, but they make an airstrike on a commander because of the protests. They don't act like they speak. This is no different from what China is doing.

SHIO OKAWA

[*Laughs.*] I see. From the opposite point of view.

MAJOR GENERAL SOLEIMANI

It's the same. China sees the Hong Kong protestors, and kills them. You know? There must be bias in Mr. Trump's sense of values.

SHIO OKAWA

Hmm. Yeah.

MAJOR GENERAL SOLEIMANI

In the religious meaning, he has bias...

SHIO OKAWA

Are Ivanka and her husband involved? Or, is it...

MAJOR GENERAL SOLEIMANI

The daughter. Umm...

SHIO OKAWA

But Mr. Trump himself seems like he has some kind of spiritual connection with Judaism (in his past life).

MAJOR GENERAL SOLEIMANI

The daughter and her husband have great influence, I guess.

"Not all Jewish think that The Islamic countries in the Middle East Should be attacked"

MAJOR GENERAL SOLEIMANI

But just because you are Jewish doesn't... There are many Jews in the U.S., but not everyone thinks that the Islamic countries in the Middle East should be attacked. Not at all.

SHIO OKAWA

You are right. There are many American Jews who are against the aggressive Israel now.

MAJOR GENERAL SOLEIMANI

And also, the tens of thousands of Iranian people in America who will be treated as terrorists.

SHIO OKAWA

Yes. There might be discrimination again.

MAJOR GENERAL SOLEIMANI

They will face many hardships... A lot of people will get arrested or get killed. I think so. You know, umm... Well, we cannot win by military power, so we can only make some kind of damage to them, I think, like shooting down an airplane, destroying a military tank, or something small, really... We can just attack something American. That's all. But the Iranian people are still angry.

3

His Current Situation

He had hoped
Iran's connection with Happy Science
Would lead to Japan's mediation

SHIO OKAWA

You were suddenly attacked by airstrike, and that is not a usual way to die. I think about a day has passed...

MAJOR GENERAL SOLEIMANI

Yeah, I think so.

SHIO OKAWA

I think you believe in the soul...

MAJOR GENERAL SOLEIMANI

Of course.

SHIO OKAWA

Right. So, how is it? Have you met any spirits?

MAJOR GENERAL SOLEIMANI

Well, there are many Middle Eastern spirits. The president and the supreme leader have been contacting Happy Science spiritually, recently, and the other day, the president said that he received Master Ryuho Okawa's gift. So, we were hoping that Japan would mediate.

SHIO OKAWA

Sorry. If we had a little more influence, we would have been able to help you.

MAJOR GENERAL SOLEIMANI

There is no reason for Japan to attack Iran. None. We believe in different religions, but we still do business, and even if we wore black clothing and said no to alcohol, the Japanese people acknowledged that as our custom and let us be. But the Americans think that everything needs to be in an American style. Everyone can drink Coca-Cola and Starbucks, that's how it needs to be. They want to make everything the same.

His deep spiritual connections with Japan

SHIO OKAWA

Do you think you can go back to heaven? In this situation...

MAJOR GENERAL SOLEIMANI

I'm like this now, so I'm not sure, but for a while, where my country is headed...

SHIO OKAWA

I'm sure you are worried.

MAJOR GENERAL SOLEIMANI

...I'm worried about it, so I cannot return so easily. But hearing me, I'm sure you know that I didn't have such an evil mind.

SHIO OKAWA

Right. You wanted to protect your country.

MAJOR GENERAL SOLEIMANI

I was a hero in Iran, you know? If I'm an evil person, then the U.S. Secretary of Defense and the CIA Director are also evil. But they are also working for their country, of course.

SHIO OKAWA

And, you can speak Japanese so fluently.

MAJOR GENERAL SOLEIMANI

Yeah. Many of us have connections with Japan.

SHIO OKAWA

Do you also?

MAJOR GENERAL SOLEIMANI

Ah, I just died, so...

SHIO OKAWA

You don't know?

MAJOR GENERAL SOLEIMANI

I cannot say too much, but I have experience as a Japanese samurai.

SHIO OKAWA

I see. Then, there must be a deep connection in your spiritual line.

MAJOR GENERAL SOLEIMANI

I think so. Elohim* had long been overseeing the Middle East. And, many Middle Eastern souls have relocated to Japan.

---

* One of the core consciousnesses of El Cantare (see p.54), the Supreme God of the Earth Spirit Group. Elohim was born about 150 million years ago, near the area that is now the Middle East, and taught teachings of wisdom, mainly on the differences of light and darkness, and good and evil. Elohim is the same being as Allah in Islam. See Ryuho Okawa, *The Laws of Faith* (New York: IRH Press, 2018).

4

Iran, an Independent Nation

Iran admitted the gap in civilization And was working on its freedom

SHIO OKAWA

What does Allah think about this?

MAJOR GENERAL SOLEIMANI

I'm sure Allah feels troubled.

SHIO OKAWA

Do God Thoth* and Allah think differently?

---

* The great religious master who led the Atlantis civilization to its golden age. He was a super genius who was a religious leader, politician, philosopher, scientist, and artist all in one. Also called the Omniscient and Omnipotent Lord Thoth. Thoth is one of the branch spirits of El Cantare, God of the Earth, and is now governing the North American Spirit World. See Ryuho Okawa, *The Laws of the Sun* (New York: IRH Press, 2018).

MAJOR GENERAL SOLEIMANI

What are we to do? To tell the truth, they are saying about the gap in our civilizations, right?

SHIO OKAWA

Right.

MAJOR GENERAL SOLEIMANI

At the time, the American and European civilizations are more superior to us. They are. The Islamic civilization used to be superior before, but now, they are more advanced as a civilization. I admit that.

SHIO OKAWA

There are aspects of the Islamic religion, itself, where progress stopped and is not compatible with the modern times. So, it needs innovation.

MAJOR GENERAL SOLEIMANI

Actually, we started on that, a little.

SHIO OKAWA

Yes, but...

MAJOR GENERAL SOLEIMANI

We started working on our freedom, but it was too slow for them, I guess. We were trying to change, but we were slow, and it made them think that killing the top leaders will be quicker.

This is almost the same as the killing of Native Americans. Americans traditionally killed Native Americans, so we are treated like them. Americans discriminate against colored people, indeed.

SHIO OKAWA

(The guardian spirit of) Mr. Khamenei said that killing the leader now will only repeat what happened in Iraq, and that it won't lead to a stable country.

MAJOR GENERAL SOLEIMANI

Because our leadership is long-term like the pope. The U.S. doesn't like that, so they want to kill the leader and make us a four-year system or term-based system where we have elections. I think so. They see that a small number of people are holding too much power.

Why did the U.S. prioritize Iran Over North Korea?

SHIO OKAWA

There is also discord between the Sunni and Shia sects.

MAJOR GENERAL SOLEIMANI

Yeah, and they took advantage of that.

SHIO OKAWA

It would have been better if there was no discord. It's might be OK to separate, but...

MAJOR GENERAL SOLEIMANI

Well, we are separate countries.

SHIO OKAWA

If there were not so much discord among the Islamic countries in the Middle East, they might have been more united, but since it is divided so much, the Western societies...

MAJOR GENERAL SOLEIMANI

So, only the Islamic countries which are pro-U.S. make so much money from their oil.

SHIO OKAWA

Ah.

MAJOR GENERAL SOLEIMANI

In the world. Those countries make great profits. But not us. It's clear. Oil is a strategic natural resource, you know?

Now, we are complaining to the United Nations that we are an independent nation and that we have the right of self-defense. The UN secretary-general agreed about that. So, they cannot say that Iran is not an independent nation.

They are thinking that if we develop nuclear energy, it will lead to our creating nuclear weapons to attack Israel. I think so. Since they cannot stop North Korea anymore, they want to act before the same thing happens. So, they are leaving North Korea for later. [*About five seconds of silence.*] They are afraid that if they do nothing, we will develop nuclear missiles. [*About five seconds of silence.*] We have oil, so we have enough in the meaning of fuel. We can get by.

SHIO OKAWA

Americans in general have hatred for the Islamic countries in the Middle East because of 9/11.

But for Japan, North Korea is close by, so it's a bigger crisis.

MAJOR GENERAL SOLEIMANI
Uh huh.

SHIO OKAWA
But if the oil stops coming from the Middle East, it's also quite a crisis.

MAJOR GENERAL SOLEIMANI
Yeah, over there. Europe is, hmm... China buys oil the most, but Europe and Japan also buy oil. We export to Asia also, so the region is still significant.

SHIO OKAWA
Hmm.

MAJOR GENERAL SOLEIMANI
The U.S. has its own resource, so I don't know what they are thinking. They want to control all the oil-

producing regions, maybe? And, the countries that Islam has spread to are all poor.

SHIO OKAWA
OK.

MAJOR GENERAL SOLEIMANI
Some oil-producing ones prospered, but the others are all poor, like the countries in Africa and Central Asia. Islam spread in many desert areas like them. They are all living in poverty, like communist countries.

Iran and Iraq have pride as great countries

SHIO OKAWA
You were born after the Iranian Revolution. Right?

MAJOR GENERAL SOLEIMANI
Yes.

SHIO OKAWA

Is that right?

MAJOR GENERAL SOLEIMANI

I think? Hmm.

SHIO OKAWA

Oh, wait...

MAJOR GENERAL SOLEIMANI

Umm, maybe not.

SHIO OKAWA

Right. I guess not.

MAJOR GENERAL SOLEIMANI

Uh huh.

SHIO OKAWA

You were active in Iran after the Iranian Revolution, but did you have some plan or purpose before you were born? I'm sorry to ask you right after you passed away.

MAJOR GENERAL SOLEIMANI

Yeah, in the spiritual or religious meaning, Iran is like Kyoto of Japan. Yeah. Iran and Iraq are to the Earth what Kyoto and Nara are to Japan.

SHIO OKAWA

Since even before Islam, right? Many religions...

MAJOR GENERAL SOLEIMANI

That's right. Actually, not Islam, but...

SHIO OKAWA

Zoroaster.

MAJOR GENERAL SOLEIMANI

No, no, no, no. Umm, Judaism.

SHIO OKAWA

Uh huh.

MAJOR GENERAL SOLEIMANI

We are continuing the Persian civilization which existed before Judaism. So, everyone thinks we are great countries. We have pride in our tradition. China says they have 5,000 years of history, but we...

SHIO OKAWA

Older.

MAJOR GENERAL SOLEIMANI

We have more than 6,000 years, definitely.

SHIO OKAWA

[*Laughs.*] True.

MAJOR GENERAL SOLEIMANI

People say that the human civilization originated in Africa, but a clear, practical civilization occurred from our region. We have pride that the religions that developed around the Tigris and Euphrates, mainly in Iran and Iraq, are the beginning of the world civilization. We think so.

SHIO OKAWA

Uh huh. I guess that's true. There is a long history.

He feels a strong bond with Japan

MAJOR GENERAL SOLEIMANI

Yeah. You are good friends with Mr. Trump, so I cannot say too much, but he doesn't know Elohim, I think.

SHIO OKAWA

It's very possible that he doesn't.

MAJOR GENERAL SOLEIMANI

We know Elohim. He is the God of the Middle East.

SHIO OKAWA

Mr. Trump doesn't know, maybe?

MAJOR GENERAL SOLEIMANI

I don't think he knows Elohim.

SHIO OKAWA

I see.

MAJOR GENERAL SOLEIMANI

Maybe he doesn't know. He doesn't know that our God is the World God.

SHIO OKAWA

You know that Allah is connected to Elohim.

MAJOR GENERAL SOLEIMANI

It's disrespectful to call Elohim by His name, directly.

SHIO OKAWA

Yes. So, you say, "Allah."

MAJOR GENERAL SOLEIMANI

So, we just call Him, "Allah."

SHIO OKAWA

Yes. OK.

MAJOR GENERAL SOLEIMANI

I know that we had connections with Japan in ancient times. We had connections with the Japanese civilization. Muhammad has connections to Japan, indeed, I know. Yeah, I know that. So, we feel a strong bond. Only if Japan had won WWII, we would have been in a quite different position. Europe would have declined, and the U.S. would have been weaker. It would have been very different.

SHIO OKAWA

But if we had won, El Cantare* may not have been born in Japan.

MAJOR GENERAL SOLEIMANI

He would have been born somehow. Some kind of...

SHIO OKAWA

He might have been persecuted.

MAJOR GENERAL SOLEIMANI

No, no. The Great Japan Co-Prosperity Sphere would have spread all over Asia, so He could have been born anywhere.

---

* The Supreme God of the Earth Spirit Group; God of the Earth who has guided humanity since the beginning of Earth and who was also involved in the Creation of the universe. The core consciousness of El Cantare has descended as "Alpha" 330 million years ago, "Elohim" 150 million years ago, and Ryuho Okawa in Japan now. See aforementioned *The Laws of the Sun* and *The Laws of Faith*.

SHIO OKAWA

You mean, it might have been better if He was born into the Imperial family?

MAJOR GENERAL SOLEIMANI

Well, He would have been careful to choose where He will be born. I have heard that you were also born in the Middle East, a long time ago.

SHIO OKAWA

Yes. Thank you.

MAJOR GENERAL SOLEIMANI

I came here right after I died. My funeral is still to come.

SHIO OKAWA

[*Laughs.*]

MAJOR GENERAL SOLEIMANI

For three days, Iran will be mourning.

SHIO OKAWA

Yes.

MAJOR GENERAL SOLEIMANI

Mourning... It's a funeral.

SHIO OKAWA

Returning to Tehran the day after tomorrow (Jan 6).

MAJOR GENERAL SOLEIMANI

Yeah, returning. I'm here giving a spiritual message even before my funeral. Sorry.

But (the guardian spirit of) Mr. Trump still cannot speak Japanese. I can speak Japanese.

SHIO OKAWA

Mr. Trump can speak simple Japanese... I guess it's because Master is the medium. But he's not as fluent as you.

MAJOR GENERAL SOLEIMANI

Yes, so you can understand how close Iran is to Japan. You know?

SHIO OKAWA

[*Laughs.*] Uh huh.

MAJOR GENERAL SOLEIMANI

It's a one-sided love.

5

The Final Goal of the U.S.

There is no Islamic country In the permanent members Of the UN Security Council

SHIO OKAWA

Then, if you have a message for Iran or Japan please...

MAJOR GENERAL SOLEIMANI

You know, the U.S. is taking the initiative. The supreme leader and the president of Iran say they will retaliate and seek for revenge, but in reality, they know that if they actually fight, they will become like Iraq.

SHIO OKAWA

Everyone knows that, right?

MAJOR GENERAL SOLEIMANI

Of course.

SHIO OKAWA

But they don't want to destroy their traditions and culture.

MAJOR GENERAL SOLEIMANI

Yeah. We should have sovereignty as an independent nation. That's what we are saying. No one supports Islamic nations in the UN... There is no Islamic country in the permanent members of the UN Security Council.

SHIO OKAWA

That's true. No permanent Islamic member.

MAJOR GENERAL SOLEIMANI

No. We are not in it.

SHIO OKAWA

It's not equal.

MAJOR GENERAL SOLEIMANI

It's not equal. If they say an Islamic nation can be dissolved in any way, we can do nothing.

SHIO OKAWA

You are right.

The reason President Trump Wants to control the Middle East

MAJOR GENERAL SOLEIMANI

If the U.S. controls the Middle East, they can kill China and Europe. They can control if China and Europe will live or die.

SHIO OKAWA

Ah. I see.

MAJOR GENERAL SOLEIMANI

If they take control of all the Middle East. Or, if they make Israel stronger and manipulate it from behind, they can rule over Europe and China. In some meaning, it means they came to take the Middle East before China takes it. If I were to speak well of the enemy.

SHIO OKAWA
Yes. Indeed.

MAJOR GENERAL SOLEIMANI
They came to take us before China did.

SHIO OKAWA
If China buys oil from Iran while they are still enemies of the U.S., and they end up joining hands, it will be quite dangerous.

MAJOR GENERAL SOLEIMANI
If Mr. Trump's final goal is to crush China, then it's important to secure the oil, of course. If the U.S. rules over the Middle East, China cannot get oil, so it's very bad for China.

SHIO OKAWA

I see.

MAJOR GENERAL SOLEIMANI

The U.S. has its own oil, coal, and natural gas, so they are OK. No problem. But it's important for them to control the Arabian area because if they do, Europe and China must listen to them. In that meaning, it's very important.

What is the meaning Behind killing Soleimani?

SHIO OKAWA

Ayatollah Khamenei will not meet with Mr. Trump...

MAJOR GENERAL SOLEIMANI

He cannot. I think so.

SHIO OKAWA

Me, too. I cannot imagine.

MAJOR GENERAL SOLEIMANI

His commander was killed by a drone. I don't think he can.

SHIO OKAWA

He will think that he will be captured.

MAJOR GENERAL SOLEIMANI

He is thinking that, next, a drone is aiming at him from above. I think so. The U.S. gave a warning that if he appears outside, like riding a car, train, or bus, they can shoot him. So, I think this means that the next time he says something offensive to the U.S., he will be assassinated.

About the helicopter crash that killed Taiwan's top military person

SHIO OKAWA

In Taiwan, a helicopter crashed, and a top military person like you was in it.

MAJOR GENERAL SOLEIMANI

I don't know so much, but they might have been targeted. I guess so.

SHIO OKAWA

Me, too.

MAJOR GENERAL SOLEIMANI

It's possible. No one might think so, but it's possible.

SHIO OKAWA

China, maybe?

MAJOR GENERAL SOLEIMANI

Nowadays, a lot of Chinese drones are flying all over the Middle East, also. So, yes, they can shoot down a helicopter. It's easier than targeting him when he is on land.

SHIO OKAWA

What do you think? Will this be war?

MAJOR GENERAL SOLEIMANI

Umm, I think it's a matter of if we will give in or not. We have pride, so I don't know if we will just surrender and say, "Our commander was defeated. We cannot fight."

Our president now used to be a military commander. He is a military person, so he cannot just do nothing. In short, the Americans in Iraq are now withdrawing, but some places that cooperated with the U.S. might be attacked, of course. I think so. Just where we can.

6

About the Upcoming War

How did the spirit of General Soleimani Come to Japan?

SHIO OKAWA

You came all the way to Japan.

MAJOR GENERAL SOLEIMANI

Yes. Thousands of kilometers. Maybe 10,000?

SHIO OKAWA

But it's only a moment as a spirit body, right?

MAJOR GENERAL SOLEIMANI

Maybe, but usually, you cannot come here in a moment.

SHIO OKAWA

What was it like coming as a spirit body? [*Laughs*].

MAJOR GENERAL SOLEIMANI

Usually, you cannot. You cannot, but it was like getting sucked through a tube and coming out on this side. "Tube" means subway in England, by the way.

SHIO OKAWA

Oh, so you were sucked in, and you came out here?

MAJOR GENERAL SOLEIMANI

Yeah. Underground tunnel of the subway, you know? It felt like I was flying in the universe. I appeared in Japan by going through a passage within the Earth.

SHIO OKAWA

OK. And, you came to Japan, or in other words, here.

MAJOR GENERAL SOLEIMANI

Yeah. Muhammad and Elohim are both in Japan.

SHIO OKAWA

Yes.

"I was killed because the U.S. Democratic Party started the impeachment trial"

SHIO OKAWA

We are very sad, also. Master is worried.

MAJOR GENERAL SOLEIMANI

But at this stage, you cannot suggest Iran to just surrender.

SHIO OKAWA

We cannot.

MAJOR GENERAL SOLEIMANI

Did we do something to deserve that? Did we invade somewhere?

SHIO OKAWA

No, you didn't at all.

MAJOR GENERAL SOLEIMANI

Mr. Trump is saying is that they were afraid of our plan to kill American people, so they prevented that by making a preemptive strike. I think so. He is saying he protected Americans by killing the commander, the person that gives orders. He is calling this defense, national defense. But is it... how do you say, acceptable? The UN will not accept it, and it will be hard to accept for the G20, really.

SHIO OKAWA

Why was it now? Oh, I guess before the sandstorm...

MAJOR GENERAL SOLEIMANI

The election, yeah, instead of the sandstorm.

SHIO OKAWA

Before the election and the sandstorm.

MAJOR GENERAL SOLEIMANI

Yeah, yeah. It's the election. Of course. The U.S. has an election this year.

SHIO OKAWA

In an evangelical church, Mr. Trump said that God is on their side.

MAJOR GENERAL SOLEIMANI

Oh, but you know, in January, Mr. Trump will be prosecuted. Impeachment trial?

SHIO OKAWA

Oh, yes.

MAJOR GENERAL SOLEIMANI

The Democrats all voted yes on the impeachment and it passed the House, and the Senate impeachment trial will start in January. But if there occurs a war, they cannot impeach him because it is their national policy, of course. So, I was killed because he was impeached. I was killed, thanks to their Democratic Party.

SHIO OKAWA

I see.

MAJOR GENERAL SOLEIMANI

So, to avoid the impeachment trial, he will make a war. Definitely.

SHIO OKAWA

Oh... Sad.

MAJOR GENERAL SOLEIMANI

He will do so to blow away the impeachment.

SHIO OKAWA

Really?

MAJOR GENERAL SOLEIMANI

And, he will try to make a lot of friends through diplomacy and surround us. We will all be called terrorists. [*Sighs.*] I don't think this will be settled, but if we lose, that's the end for us.

The U.S. cherishes their success
That came after defeating Japan

MAJOR GENERAL SOLEIMANI

Actually, after the U.S. defeated Japan, Japan recovered and became their ally, so they cherish this as their great success.

SHIO OKAWA

I see. You mean, they want Iran to be like Japan.

MAJOR GENERAL SOLEIMANI

But other times, like in Vietnam, they struggled a lot at war. The U.S. was not very successful, you know? Also, they were not successful with Korea. They succeeded with Japan only. In the end, Ayatollah Khamenei must make a vow like Emperor Hirohito did, a vow for complete obedience to the U.S., right? They are asking him to make a humanity declaration like that.

SHIO OKAWA

And, get rid of your weapons.

MAJOR GENERAL SOLEIMANI

Yeah, yeah. Complete disarmament, and "Don't turn against the U.S. or think of attacking Israel. Never." They want to do so. But we might not calm down.

SHIO OKAWA

Hmm... It's not so easy.

A war means you can be attacked
Even if you do nothing wrong

MAJOR GENERAL SOLEIMANI

It's sad. I'm sad that we cannot be your friends or be helpful to you.

SHIO OKAWA

Sorry...

MAJOR GENERAL SOLEIMANI

A commander's life is cheap. Truly, it is. A several hundred-thousand-dollar drone can kill very easily.

SHIO OKAWA

But if you are not evil-minded, you will be judged correctly in the other world. I think so.

MAJOR GENERAL SOLEIMANI

I can do nothing more. There will be a national funeral in Iran soon, but please say to everyone at Happy Science that, "A war is a fight to decide what is right and wrong, and it's quite difficult to see fairly. But please help Iran if Iran is in a tough time." It's difficult for Happy Science because you have to deal with many problems like the China, Hong Kong, Taiwan, Uyghur, and North Korea problems. You cannot give in to North Korea so easily.

SHIO OKAWA

Uh huh.

MAJOR GENERAL SOLEIMANI

Yes. Japan cannot surrender unconditionally to North Korea. You cannot, of course. No.

SHIO OKAWA

But even if we do nothing wrong, we can be attacked. This is what a war means.

MAJOR GENERAL SOLEIMANI

It's possible. Now, you know.

SHIO OKAWA

Yes.

MAJOR GENERAL SOLEIMANI

It's a disadvantage for them to fight the U.S., but they can occupy Japan if the Japan-U.S. alliance breaks. Yeah. If they say they have both atomic bombs and hydrogen bombs, they can. What will Japan do about this? Please think carefully from now on and follow the path to solution. Also, please don't abandon Iran. Thank you.

SHIO OKAWA

OK. I pray you rest in peace.

MAJOR GENERAL SOLEIMANI

Thank you. It's sad. A commander who is killed without doing anything is pitiful. I think so.

SHIO OKAWA

No, no...

7

President Trump's World Strategy

What it means to rule the Middle East

MAJOR GENERAL SOLEIMANI

I'm sorry to come at night. For his work tomorrow[*],
he was planning to give a lecture from the standpoint
of the U.S., but I came, so it's harder for him now,
maybe. I'm sorry.

SHIO OKAWA

No, no. I think that Master really understands the
U.S. standpoint and the hearts of you, the people
of Iran.

MAJOR GENERAL SOLEIMANI

The U.S. will make a lot of profit because the price
of their petroleum, natural gas, shale oil, shale gas,

---

[*] The lecture titled, "The Lecture On *The Laws of Steel*" was held at Happy
Science Tokyo Shoshinkan on January 5, 2020, the day after this spiritual
message was recorded.

and coal will go up. I think so. And, Mr. Trump will have his second term, so it's good for him. But in the end, his final strategy is to rule the Middle East, which is Europe and China's vital point. This is his world strategy. So, he's quite wise, I think.

SHIO OKAWA
OK.

General Soleimani,
A hero in his home country

MAJOR GENERAL SOLEIMANI
But you know, even someone small and weak has his own will, so they shouldn't underestimate us. If they can do it or not is... We did nothing wrong, unlike North Korea.

SHIO OKAWA
And, you have faith in God.

MAJOR GENERAL SOLEIMANI

I don't think we made terrorism so much. I can understand if we killed Americans. But now, it is being reported how many of us were killed.

SHIO OKAWA

You have deep love for your home country, but you can also see from the standpoint of the U.S. that, in the meaning of world strategy, controlling the Middle East means taking the vital point of Europe and China. I think that is truly wonderful.

MAJOR GENERAL SOLEIMANI

I was a presidential candidate, you know [*laughs*]? If I cannot see that much, I cannot be a candidate. I'm a hero in my home country.

SHIO OKAWA

I wish there were politicians like you in Japan.

MAJOR GENERAL SOLEIMANI

A hero in my home country, but a terrorist in the eyes of the U.S.

SHIO OKAWA

Hmm.

MAJOR GENERAL SOLEIMANI

So, I want to ask God to make judgment on this bias. I'm sorry, I interfered with tomorrow's event. I talked for more than 30 minutes.

SHIO OKAWA

But I think it was one of Master's major worries, so I'm glad to hear your opinion.

"Mr. Trump never misses his chance"

MAJOR GENERAL SOLEIMANI

This can be positive in the end, I think.

SHIO OKAWA

OK.

MAJOR GENERAL SOLEIMANI

The Middle East... Iran might see "flames," but China is buying the most oil from the Middle East now, and if the U.S. can control Iran, they already have control over Saudi Arabia and Iraq, so it will be difficult for China to make war.

SHIO OKAWA

Maybe they can interfere with the "One Belt, One Road" Initiative.

MAJOR GENERAL SOLEIMANI

Cut it off. The oil for Europe must go through the U.S. checkpoint, so in that meaning, Mr. Trump never misses his chance. At the same time, he's trying to kill two birds with one stone by getting rid of his impeachment trial. Now was his only chance.

SHIO OKAWA

I see.

MAJOR GENERAL SOLEIMANI

Hmm. Please give us good advice.

SHIO OKAWA

OK. It's really... OK.

MAJOR GENERAL SOLEIMANI

We are not afraid of death at all. In school, we are taught about life after death.

SHIO OKAWA

Our position and country might be different, but we can see each other in the other world if we can return to the other world with a pure heart. I think so. So, we will work hard, also.

MAJOR GENERAL SOLEIMANI

Uh huh.

8

Soleimani's Deep Connection to Japan In His Past Life

MAJOR GENERAL SOLEIMANI

I just want to say, my soul was born as a Japanese...

SHIO OKAWA

Do you know which era it was?

MAJOR GENERAL SOLEIMANI

The Kamakura period.

SHIO OKAWA

The Kamakura period?

MAJOR GENERAL SOLEIMANI

Yeah.

SHIO OKAWA

Genpei?

MAJOR GENERAL SOLEIMANI

No, I fought in Kita-Kyushu.

SHIO OKAWA

Mongol invasion?

MAJOR GENERAL SOLEIMANI

Yeah, yeah.

SHIO OKAWA

Really?

MAJOR GENERAL SOLEIMANI

I fought, in my area, against the Mongols... I was a samurai of Kyushu who fought against the allied forces of Yuan dynasty and Goryeo.

SHIO OKAWA

Then, you are always fighting to protect your country. Thank you for that.

MAJOR GENERAL SOLEIMANI

OK.

SHIO OKAWA

We think we have a heart to heart exchange with the people of Iran, so we are very sad.

MAJOR GENERAL SOLEIMANI

There are a few people who understand us even a little in Japan, and I'm glad about that. Thank you.

SHIO OKAWA

Thank you.

2

Spiritual Messages from The Guardian Spirit of Ayatollah Khamenei

Originally recorded in Japanese, on January 7, 2020
at Special Lecture Hall, Happy Science, Japan
and later translated into English

Ali Khamenei (1939 - Present)

An Iranian religious figure and politician. After studying at a seminary in Najaf, one of the holy cities of Shia Islam, he went on to study at a seminary in Qom under Khomeini. Khamenei participated in the Iranian Revolution, and after that, served posts such as a member of the council of the Islamic Revolution, the deputy defense minister, the head of revolutionary guards, and the secretary of the supreme national security council. He was elected the president of Iran in 1981, and re-elected in 1985. In 1989, after the passing of Khomeini, the first supreme leader, Khamenei became the second supreme leader of Iran.

Interviewer from Happy Science[*]

Shio Okawa
Aide to Master & CEO

[*] Her professional title represents her position at the time of the interview.

1

Iran: Dictatorship or Democracy?

The guardian spirit of Iran's supreme leader
Pays a visit in the middle of the night

KHAMENEI'S G.S.

[*Breathes heavily.*] I'm Khamenei.

SHIO OKAWA

Ayatollah Khamenei?

KHAMENEI'S G.S.

Yes. Sorry to bother you at night.

SHIO OKAWA

It's 2:30 AM. I can understand that you are struggling.

KHAMENEI'S G.S.

We are in a different time zone... Sorry to bother you so late at night.

SHIO OKAWA

No, no. Sorry.

KHAMENEI'S G.S.

I came because I thought I should pay my respects as much as I can. We consulted you, and you published our spiritual messages*, but I'm afraid your efforts ended up in vain. I'm sorry about that.

---

* See aforementioned *Iran no Hanron: Rouhani Daitoryo, Khamenei shi Shugorei, Khomeini shi no Reigen* (lit. "Iran's Counterargument: Spiritual Messages from the Guardian Spirits of President Rouhani and Ayatollah Khamenei, and the Spirit of Ayatollah Khomeini"), and *Igirisu Iran no Tenkanten ni Tsuite* (lit. "On the Turning Point of England and Iran") (both Tokyo: IRH Press, 2019).

SHIO OKAWA

Actually, we are sorry for not being able to help you Iranian people.

KHAMENEI'S G.S.

They killed Soleimani so suddenly. You said our opinion on behalf of us, and made efforts to mediate between us and the U.S. as a neutral player. And, President Trump is an important figure to you, I think, so it's not so good for you or us that our relations are not working out well. However, Soleimani was suddenly killed, in our neighbor country, and now, people in Iraq and Iran are saying, "Death to America!" It's the same with our parliament.

The U.S. is asking us to change our ways in the name of democracy because they think we are behind in civilization, but if we were to follow our people's opinion based on democracy, we will need to make some kind of retaliation to the U.S.

If not, the people will not stop. If we were just a dictatorship, I can do anything by my decision only, but we don't have such kind of system. The people are protesting, and the members of our parliament all agree on retaliation. Iran is not run by my personal opinions or totalitarianism. Everyone feels that the killing of Soleimani was a disgrace to the nation.

If the U.S. attacks with nuclear weapons, It will be a one-sided invasion

KHAMENEI'S G.S.

The U.S. is strong, but is it right to come to the other side of the world and make an independent country their servant? In addition to that, we were doing our best to follow our agreement in the nuclear deal, but they have started redeveloping their mid-range and long-range nuclear missiles. They violated the agreement (with Russia). It means they can launch missiles from the U.S. mainland or from their Fifth Fleet somewhere in the ocean.

But we don't have nuclear weapons right now. We can make guerrilla attacks from somewhere around Iran or Iraq. So, if the U.S. will attack using strategic nuclear weapons, it means they will be attacking us one-sidedly without getting a consensus from the international community.

SHIO OKAWA
Uh huh.

KHAMENEI'S G.S.
Am I wrong?

SHIO OKAWA
No, I don't think so.

The Iranian public opinion is
Now completely anti-U.S.

SHIO OKAWA

So many Iranian people are sad about Major General Soleimani's death. It's a huge matter.

KHAMENEI'S G.S.

If the U.S. doesn't feel the same as you, then it means they think we are inferior people. They see our national opinion, our anger, as a riot by inferior people or low-IQ people, completely.

SHIO OKAWA

Yeah. Even the Iranian people who were protesting against the government are now protesting against the U.S. They have changed.

KHAMENEI'S G.S.

The U.S. thought they can defeat our regime because they thought it was evil when they saw our people protesting against our government. But when they killed our commander, the Iranian public opinion became completely anti-U.S. Our people were also protesting against me, who is the supreme leader, or the president, but they were just...

SHIO OKAWA
Saying...

KHAMENEI'S G.S.
...saying their opinion in a democratic way. What is major and what is minor...

SHIO OKAWA
They know?

KHAMENEI'S G.S.
...what is important or not, they know. They were asking the government to take some kind of action, I mean, they were just asking us to do something about our poor economic activity because of

sanctions. But if the U.S. is going as far as to kill our commander, the people will not stay silent about it.

The killing of Soleimani explained from A Japanese standpoint

KHAMENEI'S G.S.

It might be different in Japan, but it's like killing Chief Cabinet Secretary Suga, using a drone, on his way to work.

SHIO OKAWA

Hmm...

KHAMENEI'S G.S.

So, I'm not sure if this issue can be resolved with talks. Americans are the terrorists, you know? It's like killing Japanese government officials, one after another, by drone attacks from U.S. bases in Japan.

They can kill Mr. Abe, too, on his way to work. They can kill the emperor, too. He commutes to work from his residence in Akasaka, right?

SHIO OKAWA
Yes.

KHAMENEI'S G.S.
He commutes from Akasaka to the Imperial Palace by car. They can target him, also. It's just one car.

SHIO OKAWA
Japanese people are peace-addicted, so...

KHAMENEI'S G.S.
No one will know.

SHIO OKAWA
No one will know what happened.

KHAMENEI'S G.S.

It's something like that.

SHIO OKAWA

OK.

KHAMENEI'S G.S.

It's like suddenly attacking the car with the imperial chrysanthemum crest on it. Or, it's like suddenly attacking the Japanese government's second or third most important person. Japan would hold a funeral and back down quietly, I think.

SHIO OKAWA

Uh huh. In Japan, there would be useless arguments, and that would be the end.

General Soleimani was loved By the Iranian people

SHIO OKAWA

On the other hand, I really thought Mr. Soleimani was loved by the Iranian people.

KHAMENEI'S G.S.

Don't you think so?

SHIO OKAWA

Yes.

KHAMENEI'S G.S.

You understood, right?

SHIO OKAWA

Yes, I did.

KHAMENEI'S G.S.

He was respected by not only the people of Iran, but by the people of Iraq, also.

SHIO OKAWA

The U.S. didn't expect Iraq to also call for the retreat of U.S. forces.

KHAMENEI'S G.S.

Soleimani was active in Iraq.

SHIO OKAWA

Uh huh.

KHAMENEI'S G.S.

He was holding together the Shia Muslims in Iraq. But it's all guerrilla forces in the eyes of the U.S. president, I guess.

SHIO OKAWA

It's a little different from killing someone like Osama bin Laden, right?

KHAMENEI'S G.S.

Yes. He was a commander chosen by due process.

SHIO OKAWA

He was an officially recognized figure by the nation.

KHAMENEI'S G.S.

He was the commander of the most elite squad directly under the supreme leader. [*About five seconds of silence.*] In terms of WWII - Japan was already in a war, but it's like killing Isoroku Yamamoto (commander-in-chief of the Combined Fleet) by airstrike in times of peace.

SHIO OKAWA

Hmm...

KHAMENEI'S G.S.

If this happened during a war, it can't be helped, I guess, but we are not at war.

2

Iran's Measures Against the U.S.

Anti-U.S. measures
By Ayatollah Khamenei's guardian spirit

SHIO OKAWA

What do you think? You have no choice but to hold out against the U.S., I guess?

KHAMENEI'S G.S.

In the end, using nuclear weapons or nuclear missiles... Considering Trump's character, he just needs to threaten us on his Twitter, "We will use strategic nuclear weapons." Then, we can do nothing, he thinks.

SHIO OKAWA

The Democratic Party is always the one giving the reason for the U.S. to go to war, although they tend to speak peace and anti-war.

KHAMENEI'S G.S.

Yes. The U.S. has already stopped reducing nuclear weapons because they need to compete with Russia and China. But they are not allowing us to use nuclear weapons. That's the condition. We were truthfully...

Of course, we cannot be satisfied with doing small-scale terrorism in Kenya. At the least, we will attack the U.S. bases in the Middle East.* We can. We will. I think so. We will attack all the U.S. embassies in the Middle East countries at the same time. I believe so. And, we can also attack the U.S. forces near the Persian Gulf. We can sink those who try to go through the Strait of Hormuz.

---

* In retaliation for the murder of Major General Soleimani, Iran fired missiles at the U.S. bases in Iraq on January 8, 2020, the day after this spiritual message was recorded.

"Mr. Trump should take responsibility For attacking under his own decision And without consensus From international society"

SHIO OKAWA

Mr. Soleimani said something like, "From the U.S. side, if they can spread their influence or power in the Middle East, they can have authority over China and Europe. This might be their strategy." (See Chapter 1.)

KHAMENEI'S G.S.

Yeah, it's true. However, I don't know if you like them or not, but China and Russia are criticizing the U.S. attacks, so we cannot speak ill of them, for now.

SHIO OKAWA

Yeah, that's true.

KHAMENEI'S G.S.

Because if they allowed such kind of attack, they could suddenly be attacked by a drone, also.

SHIO OKAWA

Master knows how the Iranian people feel, so he was in tears, I think.

KHAMENEI'S G.S.

There was some level of consensus for the coalition forces in the past, but this time, there was no consensus. It was done by Mr. Trump's own decision. He didn't get approval from Congress. I think he should take responsibility for that.

Mr. Abe is saying he will come to the Middle East, but I don't know if he can, and I don't think he can help us at all.

SHIO OKAWA

You came here as a spirit. Does anyone from the heavenly world come to give you an opinion?

KHAMENEI'S G.S.

Hmm. Umm... [*About five seconds of silence.*] Khomeini...

SHIO OKAWA

Ah.

KHAMENEI'S G.S.

And other past, old leaders of Iran. They come to me to say something.

SHIO OKAWA

What is the strongest opinion?

KHAMENEI'S G.S.

They are all saying, "Take the chance. Abandon the nuclear deal and make nuclear weapons. If not, you cannot defend against them."

The U.S. cannot occupy Iran easily

SHIO OKAWA

Then, you are planning to retaliate against the U.S. immediately...

KHAMENEI'S G.S.

Yes, we will. But if they want to fight an all-out war, there needs to be more than just several thousand troops coming at a time. They need a much bigger number of troops.

SHIO OKAWA

The U.S., you mean?

KHAMENEI'S G.S.

Yes. They cannot occupy Iran. We have hundreds of thousands of troops, so it's not so easy. And, they are making an enemy of Iraq, so it's not so easy.

Especially, General Soleimani had established Iran support forces from Yemen across some countries, in a crescent shape. Those people will not stay silent, so they will attack the U.S. bases from multiple locations. The U.S. might think they are fighting against Iran, but there will be other non-Iranians joining in the attack.

So, Saudi Arabia might not, but others will be very... Saudi Arabia and Israel might not, but other countries with Shia Muslims will attack, I think. There are many countries with Shia Muslims. They will surely attack the U.S. embassies, and attack U.S. aircraft, drones, and ships. And, of course, there will occur guerrilla activities in the Middle East, Africa, Europe, and U.S. mainland.

SHIO OKAWA

I see.

"I'm sorry that our friendship
With Happy Science ended up in vain"

KHAMENEI'S G.S.

This has become an issue between two countries, so it cannot be settled easily. I'm sorry that our friendship with you ended up in vain.

SHIO OKAWA

No, no.

KHAMENEI'S G.S.

Mr. Abe was "a mediator," but he did nothing. I expect nothing from him. I'm just sorry because you published books on behalf of Iran.

SHIO OKAWA

Master Okawa was very sad because we didn't have enough power. He said he was sorry. Lord Elohim*

and others think Islam needs some kind of reform, but they are sad about an all-out war, I think.

---

* See p.39.

3

The Reality of Iran and
The Prejudice of Americans

Iran is a legitimate nation, unlike Al-Qaeda

KHAMENEI'S G.S.

CNN is reporting on anti-U.S. protest in Iran, but the Iranian people don't want to kill CNN people just because they are American.

SHIO OKAWA

Yes.

KHAMENEI'S G.S.

Our people are rational enough, you know?

SHIO OKAWA

So, Americans have a strong image of people like Al-Qaeda and ISIS...

KHAMENEI'S G.S.

Yeah, they think we are all the same.

SHIO OKAWA

Yeah. Other countries also thought Iran was the same, but this time...

KHAMENEI'S G.S.

We are a legitimate nation.

SHIO OKAWA

Uh huh. You are a legitimate nation, and your commanders and top-level people are respected and loved so much by the people.

KHAMENEI'S G.S.

The U.S. assassinated him, they killed him in Iraq. This means they think Iraq is a part of the U.S. I think so.

President Trump's judgment:
Major General Soleimani is the mastermind

SHIO OKAWA

But Mr. Trump is smart about... It might sound rude, but I thought he changed his thinking regarding the Middle East, a little.

KHAMENEI'S G.S.

Well, he attacked a few... It was out of the blue, not a large-scale military order. He saw about 4,700 Iraq people protesting at the U.S. embassy in Iraq, and ordered an attack. He thought they were being lured to do that, but it was the will of the Iraq people.

SHIO OKAWA

Yes. The mastermind behind it...

KHAMENEI'S G.S.

Yeah, yeah, yeah. Soleimani...

SHIO OKAWA

He thought Mr. Soleimani was making them do it.

KHAMENEI'S G.S.

He thought Soleimani was making them do it, so he had to kill. That's his way of thinking from the beginning. The president judged that Soleimani did everything, like attacking using drones, attacking tanks, and attacking ships. [*Sighs.*]

SHIO OKAWA

In the past, there was a protest at a U.S. Embassy, and four Americans died. He didn't want the same thing to happen again, so he bombed six people, including Mr. Soleimani, when they were riding in a car, I think.

America's most hard-liners believe Islam To be devil's teachings

KHAMENEI'S G.S.

The attack on World Trade Center was done by Saudi Arabians, but the U.S. hated Iraq and invaded it. In the end, they killed Osama bin Laden in Afghanistan, I mean, not Afghanistan, but Pakistan. They did.

SHIO OKAWA

Yes.

KHAMENEI'S G.S.

This time, they say Iran is a terrorist, but we have a religion and we are running a form of democracy.

SHIO OKAWA

I think they are confused. And speaking of Pakistan, for example, Ms. Malala (Yousafzai)said strongly to give education to women, and terrorists attacked her. Now, she's in England.

KHAMENEI'S G.S.

The most hard-liners' opinion is that Iraq and Iran... They believe Islam is devil's teachings. I think so.

SHIO OKAWA

From the standpoint of the U.S., you mean?

KHAMENEI'S G.S.

Fundamentally. They think so. Maybe.

SHIO OKAWA

"Bring home devils from places like Iraq, and experience terrible things." American horror movies are like that.

KHAMENEI'S G.S.

Yeah, that's right. But instead, this is making

terrorists of Iranian people. Because if Iranian people in the U.S. are thought as terrorists, they cannot stay there, so they will have to do something. They will be expelled from the U.S. soon, but it's a false accusation. They are victims.

4

Relationship Between Iran and the U.S., And Between Iran and Japan

The guardian spirits of Ayatollah Khamenei And President Trump are not fighting

SHIO OKAWA

The guardian spirit of Mr. Trump doesn't come to you?

KHAMENEI'S G.S.

Not at all.

SHIO OKAWA

OK. It's not a personal fight, so I can understand.

KHAMENEI'S G.S.

We are both... Fight... No. You think highly of Trump, so I'm sorry.

SHIO OKAWA

We don't agree with Mr. Trump or praise him about everything. When Master has his own opinion, he clearly says so in his lectures.

KHAMENEI'S G.S.

Now, anti-U.S. movements are making a great comeback in the Middle East. If this is what Trump wanted, it cannot be helped... How many people he wants to kill, I don't know.

SHIO OKAWA

Who is a hard-liner who can speak his opinion to Mr. Trump... There is a hard-liner, I guess.

KHAMENEI'S G.S.

Trump fired Bolton. It might be his thinking...

SHIO OKAWA

Close to his thinking.

KHAMENEI'S G.S.

Close, right? "It's hopeless. It's devil's teachings, so we have to destroy it." That's his thinking from the beginning.

SHIO OKAWA

Hmm.

KHAMENEI'S G.S.

The attack was almost exactly like such thinking. So, he thinks there is no room for negotiation, not even as much as with North Korea.

"We don't expect to live much longer"

KHAMENEI'S G.S.

[*Sighs.*] There will occur a war, I guess. But we will be targeted even though we are in the middle of a funeral, I think. Sorry. You were supporting us.

SHIO OKAWA

No, no. We are really...

KHAMENEI'S G.S.

We cannot stop it, maybe. So, we don't expect to live much longer. They think this will end if they kill the top, but they need to know that it's a misunderstanding.

SHIO OKAWA

We hope they will understand that.

KHAMENEI'S G.S.

They think we are dictating. They think we are dictators.

Japan is peace-addicted
And in a different group of its own

SHIO OKAWA

There were so many people (protesting). We don't see something like that in Japan. Very few.

KHAMENEI'S G.S.

Even if a Japanese minister is killed, Japanese people will not say to retaliate. I don't think so.

SHIO OKAWA

Maybe not. They might be lost and not know what is going on... And, they will argue about the constitution again. That will be all.

KHAMENEI'S G.S.

Japan is in a little different group of its own.

SHIO OKAWA

They won't know that it's such a big issue.

KHAMENEI'S G.S.

Because they are peace-addicted.

SHIO OKAWA

Yes.

If China and Russia assist Iran, There might occur a world war

KHAMENEI'S G.S.

We don't have nuclear weapons, but we have missiles. And, if China or Russia or North Korea assists us, we can get nuclear weapons.

SHIO OKAWA

Uh huh.

KHAMENEI'S G.S.

There can occur a world war. It's possible, if China and Russia join in this war. So, we are at a very dangerous stage now. And, Happy Science and Mr. Abe, you can do almost nothing. Trump decided to attack while Mr. Abe was playing golf. [*Sighs.*]

SHIO OKAWA

He was asked to mediate, but Mr. Trump didn't consult him.

KHAMENEI'S G.S.

It was just... He just wanted to look like a good guy. The U.S. is "a dictatorship," not us. The U.S. president has many aspects of a dictator. It means Mr. Trump wants the U.S. to be strong, that's all. I think so.

5

Understanding Iranian Culture and Custom

Iran places importance on obedience

SHIO OKAWA

When you visit us, it's far, but how do you come? Are you praying?

KHAMENEI'S G.S.

Ah. Hmm.

SHIO OKAWA

Or, did you come today because we had spiritual conversations and you wanted to talk to Master?

KHAMENEI'S G.S.

We place importance on obedience. We want to say sorry because there might occur a war even though

El Cantare tried to stop us, and we want Him to understand our feelings.

SHIO OKAWA

El Cantare said He couldn't do anything for the Iranian people, and was running a lot of tears, I think. So, I hope His feelings reach you.

KHAMENEI'S G.S.

We, the Iranian leaders, might be called mad dictators, but if killing us will lead to a democratic, free, and modern Iran, please do so.

SHIO OKAWA

Hmm.

KHAMENEI'S G.S.

Having the U.S. forces make territories and march through Iran, occupying it and claiming that they freed the people. Is that such a good future? All of the Islamic countries have hatred for Israel, you know? The U.S. "gave" the Golan Heights to Israel, and admitted their expansionism. And, Iran was the strongest deterrent for that. The U.S. wants to make all Islamic countries second or third rate nations and make us a group under Christianity. I think so.

SHIO OKAWA

Such kind of mistake has been continuing from the Bush administration.

KHAMENEI'S G.S.

Uh huh.

SHIO OKAWA

They didn't identify the criminal, and also attacked Iraq, so they are attracting a lot of hatred and disgust, even more.

KHAMENEI'S G.S.

The criminals of terrorism in the U.S. were people who lived there. So, black... the people with black wear all look like devils to them. So, there is a high possibility of a war soon. Mr. Trump will not apologize. I think so.

Islamic women's black wear is A custom of the desert area

SHIO OKAWA

What if women stopped wearing black? What do you think?

KHAMENEI'S G.S.

The sun is strong here. They are just wearing it because it's a custom.

SHIO OKAWA

The sun is strong, and how do you say, when the prophet Muhammad was alive, in the beginning of Islam, not all women were dressed like that, I think. It was a custom that started sometime in its history.

There were many incidents, I guess. I was thinking that maybe this custom started from the feelings of men living in this world.

KHAMENEI'S G.S.

It's a custom seen widely in the desert area, including Central Asia.

SHIO OKAWA

But Christian nuns are also dressed like that.

KHAMENEI'S G.S.

It's like banning Japanese people from wearing kimono, really.

SHIO OKAWA

Like that.

KHAMENEI'S G.S.

They are free to Westernize. Hmm.

SHIO OKAWA

Some women are opposing such custom, for example, Iranian female writers who are publishing books in the West.

KHAMENEI'S G.S.

A lot of American businesspeople, TV stars, and politicians would get a death sentence if they were in an Islamic country. The U.S. wants us to give freedom, not death sentence, regarding all that these people do. But it means the U.S. will attack the teachings of Islam, I think.

SHIO OKAWA

Hmm. It's difficult.

6

A Message to Japan and the World

Asking Japan to suggest a ceasefire
If Iran goes to war against the U.S.

KHAMENEI'S G.S.

So, from tomorrow...

SHIO OKAWA

The funeral ends.

KHAMENEI'S G.S.

We will start a war, I think. Sorry. Please suggest a ceasefire at some point, so that Iran will not be totally destroyed.

SHIO OKAWA

OK.

KHAMENEI'S G.S.

I might not be alive at that time, so I ask you. OK.
I will come to Allah.

SHIO OKAWA

Words cannot describe this feeling, really. May
Allah bless you.

KHAMENEI'S G.S.

We have pride, but it's not for a dictatorship. It's
our honor to our long culture and history. But they
don't understand that. Yeah.

SHIO OKAWA

The Western societies, I mean the U.S. and Europe,
are not all good.

KHAMENEI'S G.S.

Things are going wrong with them now.

SHIO OKAWA

The Iranian female writer, in her book, she said... She wants Iran to Westernize, I guess, but she got depressed after going to Europe and seeing drugs and sexually wild people. So, I can understand that you don't want such kind of things coming into Iran.

KHAMENEI'S G.S.

[*Sighs.*]

SHIO OKAWA

It's OK if the good parts of cultures are passed down.

KHAMENEI'S G.S.

How do you say, the final cleanup? When the time comes to make peace, there will be no one who can make the decision, I think, so I ask Japan to do it. Please.

SHIO OKAWA

OK.

KHAMENEI'S G.S.

If there occurs a war, and if they come to us aggressively, it will end by spring. I think so. If everyone sees our presidential palace burned to nothing, they will know. But the Tokyo Olympics will be a far-off dream.

SHIO OKAWA

Where can we find peace? It's not so easy to understand different cultures.

KHAMENEI'S G.S.

Please explain wisely.

SHIO OKAWA

OK.

The U.S. should be prepared
To suffer losses of war

KHAMENEI'S G.S.

We are ready to die at any time, yeah. If we are not allowed to fight, then it means we have no right to self-defend our nation. UN Secretary-General António Guterres said we have the right of self-defense, so we did nothing wrong in international law.

SHIO OKAWA

Yes. Iran is right as a country to...

KHAMENEI'S G.S.

Mr. Trump was thinking that if he threatened us, we will surrender. I know they have a great military. But if they are going to send many soldiers to the desert region, they must be prepared to suffer some losses in our home field.

SHIO OKAWA

Hmm.

KHAMENEI'S G.S.

The U.S. has made the same mistake, again and again.

Iranian supreme leader's heartfelt wish

SHIO OKAWA

I'm sorry if this sounds rude, but when I spoke with Mr. Soleimani, I think he felt something similar to what the Japanese generals* felt during the Battle of Iwo Jima or Okinawa in WWII. I felt so. He had to defend...

---

* See Ryuho Okawa, *The Battle of Iwo Jima: A Memoir of Japanese General Tadamichi Kuribayashi* and *For the Love of the Country: Untold Story of the Battle of Peleliu: a Memoir of Japanese Colonel Kunio Nakagawa* (both Tokyo: HS Press, 2015).

KHAMENEI'S G.S.

They can kill a military figure, but there are replacements, so there will be a new commander, one after another. A new supreme leader and a new president, also, can be elected if they are killed. So, if they think we are dictators...

SHIO OKAWA

They are wrong, you mean.

KHAMENEI'S G.S.

They should know that we have many replacement "Hitlers".

SHIO OKAWA

Completely different from Kim Jong-un.

KHAMENEI'S G.S.

There's no one to replace him over there, right?

SHIO OKAWA

No.

KHAMENEI'S G.S.

But we do. Some people protested and told me to resign because it's difficult for them to live. Anyway, it will start soon. Please settle things, so that the Iranian people will not suffer for a long time. I ask you.

SHIO OKAWA

Thank you for coming.

KHAMENEI'S G.S.

Yes. Sorry. Sorry for coming at night.

SHIO OKAWA

No, don't be. Thank you very much.

Afterword

Last year, Happy Science published a Japanese-translated version of the book, *Trumponomics**, which reveals the secret of President Trump's economic success. On the other hand, we also published books such as *Iran's Counterargument* last year, and have been working to mediate a peace talk between the U.S. and Iran's Ayatollah Khamenei and President Rouhani.

Soon after that, Major General Soleimani was killed and Iran made a counterattack to the U.S. bases. This is truly sad. I don't wish for any war among believers of God. And, I believe it is my mission to explain the difference between beliefs.

General Soleimani is a noble spirit. Also, it is true that President Trump is one of God's messengers. He was sent to this world to rebuild America.

---

* *Trumponomics* (Tokyo: IRH Press, 2019)

It is the mission of Happy Science to create peace in the world. I strongly believe so. We must have "the mind of steel."

Ryuho Okawa
Master & CEO of Happy Science Group
Jan. 10, 2020

ABOUT THE AUTHOR

Founder and CEO of Happy Science Group.

Ryuho Okawa was born on July 7th 1956, in Tokushima, Japan. After graduating from the University of Tokyo with a law degree, he joined a Tokyo-based trading house. While working at its New York headquarters, he studied international finance at the Graduate Center of the City University of New York. In 1981, he attained Great Enlightenment and became aware that he is El Cantare with a mission to bring salvation to all humankind.

In 1986, he established Happy Science. It now has members in over 165 countries across the world, with more than 700 branches and temples as well as 10,000 missionary houses around the world.

He has given over 3,400 lectures (of which more than 150 are in English) and published over 3,000 books (of which more than 600 are Spiritual Interview Series), and many are translated into 40 languages. Along with *The Laws of the Sun* and *The Laws Of Messiah*, many of the books have become best sellers or million sellers. To date, Happy Science has produced 25 movies. The original story and original concept were given by the Executive Producer Ryuho Okawa. He has also composed music and written lyrics of over 450 pieces.

Moreover, he is the Founder of Happy Science University and Happy Science Academy (Junior and Senior High School), Founder and President of the Happiness Realization Party, Founder and Honorary Headmaster of Happy Science Institute of Government and Management, Founder of IRH Press Co., Ltd., and the Chairperson of NEW STAR PRODUCTION Co., Ltd. and ARI Production Co., Ltd.

WHAT IS EL CANTARE?

El Cantare means "the Light of the Earth," and is the Supreme God of the Earth who has been guiding humankind since the beginning of Genesis. He is whom Jesus called Father and Muhammad called Allah, and is *Ame-no-Mioya-Gami*, Japanese Father God. Different parts of El Cantare's core consciousness have descended to Earth in the past, once as Alpha and another as Elohim. His branch spirits, such as Shakyamuni Buddha and Hermes, have descended to Earth many times and helped to flourish many civilizations. To unite various religions and to integrate various fields of study in order to build a new civilization on Earth, a part of the core consciousness has descended to Earth as Master Ryuho Okawa.

Alpha is a part of the core consciousness of El Cantare who descended to Earth around 330 million years ago. Alpha preached Earth's Truths to harmonize and unify Earth-born humans and space people who came from other planets.

Elohim is a part of El Cantare's core consciousness who descended to Earth around 150 million years ago. He gave wisdom, mainly on the differences of light and darkness, good and evil.

Ame-no-Mioya-Gami (Japanese Father God) is the Creator God and the Father God who appears in the ancient literature, *Hotsuma Tsutae*. It is believed that He descended on the foothills of Mt. Fuji about 30,000 years ago and built the Fuji dynasty, which is the root of the Japanese civilization. With justice as the central pillar, Ame-no-Mioya-Gami's teachings spread to ancient civilizations of other countries in the world.

Shakyamuni Buddha was born as a prince into the Shakya Clan in India around 2,600 years ago. When he was 29 years old, he renounced the world and sought enlightenment. He later attained Great Enlightenment and founded Buddhism.

Hermes is one of the 12 Olympian gods in Greek mythology, but the spiritual Truth is that he taught the teachings of love and progress around 4,300 years ago that became the origin of the current Western civilization. He is a hero that truly existed.

Ophealis was born in Greece around 6,500 years ago and was the leader who took an expedition to as far as Egypt. He is the God of miracles, prosperity, and arts, and is known as Osiris in the Egyptian mythology.

Rient Arl Croud was born as a king of the ancient Incan Empire around 7,000 years ago and taught about the mysteries of the mind. In the heavenly world, he is responsible for the interactions that take place between various planets.

Thoth was an almighty leader who built the golden age of the Atlantic civilization around 12,000 years ago. In the Egyptian mythology, he is known as god Thoth.

Ra Mu was a leader who built the golden age of the civilization of Mu around 17,000 years ago. As a religious leader and a politician, he ruled by uniting religion and politics.

WHAT IS A SPIRITUAL MESSAGE?

We are all spiritual beings living on this earth. The following is the mechanism behind Master Ryuho Okawa's spiritual messages.

1 You are a spirit

People are born into this world to gain wisdom through various experiences and return to the other world when their lives end. We are all spirits and repeat this cycle in order to refine our souls.

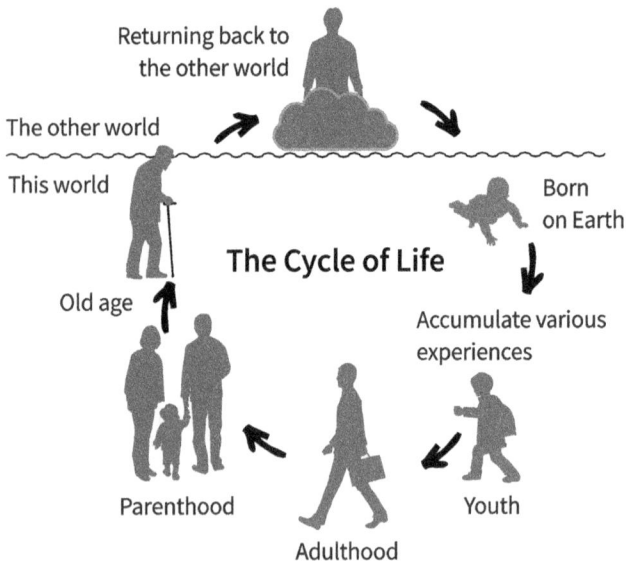

Returning back to
the other world

The other world

This world

Born
on Earth

The Cycle of Life

Old age

Accumulate various
experiences

Parenthood

Adulthood

Youth

2 You have a guardian spirit

Guardian spirits are those who protect the people who are living on this earth. Each of us has a guardian spirit that watches over us and guides us from the other world. They were us in our past life, and are identical in how we think.

The other world

This world

Guardian Spirit

Watches over us/
sends us inspiration

You

3 How spiritual messages work

Master Ryuho Okawa, through his enlightenment, is capable of summoning any spirit from anywhere in the world, including the spirit world.

Master Okawa's way of receiving spiritual messages is fundamentally different from that of other psychic mediums who undergo trances and are thereby completely taken over by the spirits they are channeling.

Master Okawa's attainment of a high level of enlightenment enables him to retain full control of his consciousness and body throughout the duration of the spiritual message. To allow the spirits to express their own thoughts and personalities freely, however, Master Okawa usually softens the dominancy of his consciousness. This way, he is able to keep his own philosophies out of the way and ensure that the spiritual messages are pure expressions of the spirits he is channeling.

Since guardian spirits think at the same subconscious level as the person living on earth, Master Okawa can summon the spirit and find out what the person on earth is actually thinking. If the person has already returned to the other world, the spirit can give messages to the people living on earth through Master Okawa.

Since 2009, many spiritual messages have been openly recorded by Master Okawa and published. Spiritual messages from the guardian spirits of people living today such as Donald Trump, former Japanese Prime Minister Shinzo Abe and Chinese President Xi Jinping, as well as spiritual messages sent from the spirit world by Jesus Christ, Muhammad, Thomas Edison, Mother Teresa, Steve Jobs and Nelson Mandela are just a tiny pack of spiritual messages that were published so far.

Domestically, in Japan, these spiritual messages are being read by a wide range of politicians and mass media, and the high-level contents of these books are delivering an impact even more on politics, news and public opinion. In recent years, there have been spiritual messages recorded in English, and

English translations are being done on the spiritual messages given in Japanese. These have been published overseas, one after another, and have started to shake the world.

① The guardian spirit / spirit in the other world...

② Goes inside Master Okawa in this world

③ Master Okawa speaks the words of the guardian spirit / spirit

For more about spiritual messages and a complete list of books in the Spiritual Interview Series, visit okawabooks.com

ABOUT HAPPY SCIENCE

Happy Science is a global movement that empowers individuals to find purpose and spiritual happiness and to share that happiness with their families, societies, and the world. With more than 12 million members around the world, Happy Science aims to increase awareness of spiritual truths and expand our capacity for love, compassion, and joy so that together we can create the kind of world we all wish to live in.

Activities at Happy Science are based on the Principle of Happiness (Love, Wisdom, Self-Reflection, and Progress). This principle embraces worldwide philosophies and beliefs, transcending boundaries of culture and religions.

Love teaches us to give ourselves freely without expecting anything in return; it encompasses giving, nurturing, and forgiving.

Wisdom leads us to the insights of spiritual truths, and opens us to the true meaning of life and the will of God (the universe, the highest power, Buddha).

Self-Reflection brings a mindful, nonjudgmental lens to our thoughts and actions to help us find our truest selves—the essence of our souls—and deepen our connection to the highest power. It helps us attain a clean and peaceful mind and leads us to the right life path.

Progress emphasizes the positive, dynamic aspects of our spiritual growth—actions we can take to manifest and spread happiness around the world. It's a path that not only expands our soul growth, but also furthers the collective potential of the world we live in.

PROGRAMS AND EVENTS

The doors of Happy Science are open to all. We offer a variety of programs and events, including self-exploration and self-growth programs, spiritual seminars, meditation and contemplation sessions, study groups, and book events.

Our programs are designed to:
* Deepen your understanding of your purpose and meaning in life
* Improve your relationships and increase your capacity to love unconditionally
* Attain peace of mind, decrease anxiety and stress, and feel positive
* Gain deeper insights and a broader perspective on the world
* Learn how to overcome life's challenges
  ... and much more.

For more information, visit happy-science.org.

OUR ACTIVITIES

Happy Science does other various activities to provide support for those in need.

◆ You Are An Angel! General Incorporated Association

Happy Science has a volunteer network in Japan that encourages and supports children with disabilities as well as their parents and guardians.

◆ Never Mind School for Truancy

At 'Never Mind,' we support students who find it very challenging to attend schools in Japan. We also nurture their self-help spirit and power to rebound against obstacles in life based on Master Okawa's teachings and faith.

◆ "Prevention Against Suicide" Campaign since 2003

A nationwide campaign to reduce suicides; over 20,000 people commit suicide every year in Japan. "The Suicide Prevention Website-Words of Truth for You-" presents spiritual prescriptions for worries such as depression, lost love, extramarital affairs, bullying and work-related problems, thereby saving many lives.

◆ Support for Anti-bullying Campaigns

Happy Science provides support for a group of parents and guardians, Network to Protect Children from Bullying, a general incorporated foundation launched in Japan to end bullying, including those that can even be called a criminal offense. So far, the network received more than 5,000 cases and resolved 90% of them.

- **The Golden Age Scholarship**

This scholarship is granted to students who can contribute greatly and bring a hopeful future to the world.

- **Success No.1**
  Buddha's Truth Afterschool Academy

Happy Science has over 180 classrooms throughout Japan and in several cities around the world that focus on afterschool education for children. The education focuses on faith and morals in addition to supporting children's school studies.

- **Angel Plan V**

For children under the age of kindergarten, Happy Science holds classes for nurturing healthy, positive, and creative boys and girls.

- **Future Stars Training Department**

The Future Stars Training Department was founded within the Happy Science Media Division with the goal of nurturing talented individuals to become successful in the performing arts and entertainment industry.

- **NEW STAR PRODUCTION Co., Ltd.**
  ARI Production Co., Ltd.

We have companies to nurture actors and actresses, artists, and vocalists. They are also involved in film production.

CONTACT INFORMATION

Happy Science is a worldwide organization with branches and temples around the globe. For a comprehensive list, visit the worldwide directory at *happy-science.org*. The following are some of the many Happy Science locations:

UNITED STATES AND CANADA

New York
79 Franklin St., New York, NY 10013, USA
Phone: 1-212-343-7972
Fax: 1-212-343-7973
Email: ny@happy-science.org
Website: happyscience-usa.org

New Jersey
66 Hudson St., #2R, Hoboken, NJ 07030, USA
Phone: 1-201-313-0127
Email: nj@happy-science.org
Website: happyscience-usa.org

Chicago
2300 Barrington Rd., Suite #400,
Hoffman Estates, IL 60169, USA
Phone: 1-630-937-3077
Email: chicago@happy-science.org
Website: happyscience-usa.org

Florida
5208 8th St., Zephyrhills, FL 33542, USA
Phone: 1-813-715-0000
Fax: 1-813-715-0010
Email: florida@happy-science.org
Website: happyscience-usa.org

Atlanta
1874 Piedmont Ave., NE Suite 360-C
Atlanta, GA 30324, USA
Phone: 1-404-892-7770
Email: atlanta@happy-science.org
Website: happyscience-usa.org

San Francisco
525 Clinton St.
Redwood City, CA 94062, USA
Phone & Fax: 1-650-363-2777
Email: sf@happy-science.org
Website: happyscience-usa.org

Los Angeles
1590 E. Del Mar Blvd., Pasadena, CA
91106, USA
Phone: 1-626-395-7775
Fax: 1-626-395-7776
Email: la@happy-science.org
Website: happyscience-usa.org

Orange County
16541 Gothard St. Suite 104
Huntington Beach, CA 92647
Phone: 1-714-659-1501
Email: oc@happy-science.org
Website: happyscience-usa.org

San Diego
7841 Balboa Ave. Suite #202
San Diego, CA 92111, USA
Phone: 1-626-395-7775
Fax: 1-626-395-7776
E-mail: sandiego@happy-science.org
Website: happyscience-usa.org

Hawaii
Phone: 1-808-591-9772
Fax: 1-808-591-9776
Email: hi@happy-science.org
Website: happyscience-usa.org

Kauai
3343 Kanakolu Street, Suite 5
Lihue, HI 96766, USA
Phone: 1-808-822-7007
Fax: 1-808-822-6007
Email: kauai-hi@happy-science.org
Website: happyscience-usa.org

Toronto
845 The Queensway
Etobicoke, ON M8Z 1N6, Canada
Phone: 1-416-901-3747
Email: toronto@happy-science.org
Website: happy-science.ca

Vancouver
#201-2607 East 49th Avenue,
Vancouver, BC, V5S 1J9, Canada
Phone: 1-604-437-7735
Fax: 1-604-437-7764
Email: vancouver@happy-science.org
Website: happy-science.ca

INTERNATIONAL

Tokyo
1-6-7 Togoshi, Shinagawa,
Tokyo, 142-0041, Japan
Phone: 81-3-6384-5770
Fax: 81-3-6384-5776
Email: tokyo@happy-science.org
Website: happy-science.org

Seoul
74, Sadang-ro 27-gil,
Dongjak-gu, Seoul, Korea
Phone: 82-2-3478-8777
Fax: 82-2-3478-9777
Email: korea@happy-science.org
Website: happyscience-korea.org

London
3 Margaret St.
London, W1W 8RE United Kingdom
Phone: 44-20-7323-9255
Fax: 44-20-7323-9344
Email: eu@happy-science.org
Website: www.happyscience-uk.org

Taipei
No. 89, Lane 155, Dunhua N. Road,
Songshan District, Taipei City 105, Taiwan
Phone: 886-2-2719-9377
Fax: 886-2-2719-5570
Email: taiwan@happy-science.org
Website: happyscience-tw.org

Sydney
516 Pacific Highway, Lane Cove North,
2066 NSW, Australia
Phone: 61-2-9411-2877
Fax: 61-2-9411-2822
Email: sydney@happy-science.org

Kuala Lumpur
No 22A, Block 2, Jalil Link Jalan Jalil
Jaya 2, Bukit Jalil 57000,
Kuala Lumpur, Malaysia
Phone: 60-3-8998-7877
Fax: 60-3-8998-7977
Email: malaysia@happy-science.org
Website: happyscience.org.my

Sao Paulo
Rua. Domingos de Morais 1154,
Vila Mariana, Sao Paulo SP
CEP 04010-100, Brazil
Phone: 55-11-5088-3800
Email: sp@happy-science.org
Website: happyscience.com.br

Kathmandu
Kathmandu Metropolitan City,
Ward No. 15, Ring Road, Kimdol,
Sitapaila Kathmandu, Nepal
Phone: 977-1-427-2931
Email: nepal@happy-science.org

Jundiai
Rua Congo, 447, Jd. Bonfiglioli
Jundiai-CEP, 13207-340, Brazil
Phone: 55-11-4587-5952
Email: jundiai@happy-science.org

Kampala
Plot 877 Rubaga Road, Kampala
P.O. Box 34130 Kampala, UGANDA
Phone: 256-79-4682-121
Email: uganda@happy-science.org

ABOUT HAPPINESS REALIZATION PARTY

The Happiness Realization Party (HRP) was founded in May 2009 by Master Ryuho Okawa as part of the Happy Science Group. HRP strives to improve the Japanese society, based on three basic political principles of "freedom, democracy, and faith," and let Japan promote individual and public happiness from Asia to the world as a leader nation.

1) Diplomacy and Security: Protecting Freedom, Democracy, and Faith of Japan and the World from China's Totalitarianism

Japan's current defense system is insufficient against China's expanding hegemony and the threat of North Korea's nuclear missiles. Japan, as the leader of Asia, must strengthen its defense power and promote strategic diplomacy together with the nations which share the values of freedom, democracy, and faith. Further, HRP aims to realize world peace under the leadership of Japan, the nation with the spirit of religious tolerance.

2) Economy: Early economic recovery through utilizing the "wisdom of the private sector"

Economy has been damaged severely by the novel coronavirus originated in China. Many companies have been forced into bankruptcy or out of business. What is needed for economic recovery now is not subsidies and regulations by the government, but policies which can utilize the "wisdom of the private sector."

For more information, visit en.hr-party.jp

ABOUT HS PRESS

HS Press is an imprint of IRH Press Co., Ltd. IRH Press Co., Ltd., based in Tokyo, was founded in 1987 as a publishing division of Happy Science. IRH Press publishes religious and spiritual books, journals, magazines and also operates broadcast and film production enterprises. For more information, visit *okawabooks.com*.

Follow us on:

f Facebook: Okawa Books   Instagram: OkawaBooks

▶ Youtube: Okawa Books   Twitter: Okawa Books

𝓟 Pinterest: Okawa Books   g Goodreads: Ryuho Okawa

---------- **NEWSLETTER** ----------

To receive book related news, promotions and events, please subscribe to our newsletter below.

⊘ eepurl.com/bsMeJj

 ---------- **AUDIO / VISUAL MEDIA** ----------

YOUTUBE   **PODCAST**

Introduction of Ryuho Okawa's titles; topics ranging from self-help, current affairs, spirituality, religion, and the universe.

BOOKS BY RYUHO OKAWA

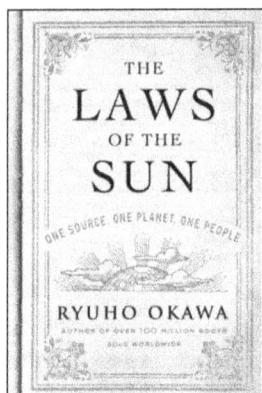

THE LAWS OF THE SUN
ONE SOURCE, ONE PLANET, ONE PEOPLE

Paperback • 288 pages • $15.95
ISBN: 978-1-942125-43-3

IMAGINE IF YOU COULD ASK GOD why He created this world and what spiritual laws He used to shape us—and everything around us. If we could understand His designs and intentions, we could discover what our goals in life should be and whether our actions move us closer to those goals or farther away.

At a young age, a spiritual calling prompted Ryuho Okawa to outline what he innately understood to be universal truths for all humankind. In *The Laws of the Sun*, Okawa outlines these laws of the universe and provides a road map for living one's life with greater purpose and meaning.

In this powerful book, Ryuho Okawa reveals the transcendent nature of consciousness and the secrets of our multidimensional universe and our place in it. By understanding the different stages of love and following the Buddhist Eightfold Path, he believes we can speed up our eternal process of development. *The Laws of the Sun* shows the way to realize true happiness—a happiness that continues from this world through the other.

For a complete list of books, visit okawabooks.com

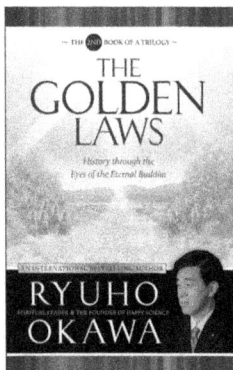

THE GOLDEN LAWS

HISTORY THROUGH THE EYES OF THE ETERNAL BUDDHA

Paperback • 201 pages • $14.95
ISBN: 978-1-941779-81-1

Throughout history, Great Guiding Spirits of Light have been present on Earth in both the East and the West at crucial points in human history to further our spiritual development. *The Golden Laws* reveals how Divine Plan has been unfolding on Earth, and outlines 5,000 years of the secret history of humankind. Once we understand the true course of history, through past, present and into the future, we cannot help but become aware of the significance of our spiritual mission in the present age.

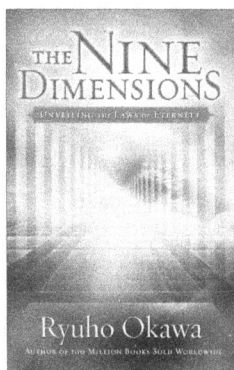

THE NINE DIMENSIONS

UNVEILING THE LAWS OF ETERNITY

Paperback • 168 pages • $15.95
ISBN: 978-0-982698-56-3

This book is a window into the mind of our loving God, who designed this world and the vast, wondrous world of our afterlife as a school with many levels through which our souls learn and grow. When the religions and cultures of the world discover the truth of their common spiritual origin, they will be inspired to accept their differences, come together under faith in God, and build an era of harmony and peaceful progress on Earth.

For a complete list of books, visit okawabooks.com

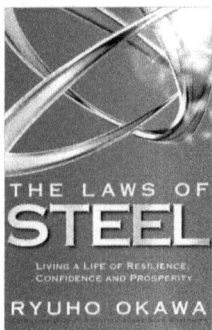

THE LAWS OF STEEL
LIVING A LIFE OF RESILIENCE, CONFIDENCE AND PROSPERITY

Paperback • 264 pages • $16.95
ISBN: 978-1-942125-65-5

This book is a compilation of six lectures that Ryuho Okawa gave in 2018 and 2019, each containing passionate messages for us to open a brighter future. This powerful and inspiring book will not only show us the ways to achieve true happiness and prosperity, but also the ways to solve many global issues we now face.

LOVE FOR THE FUTURE
BUILDING ONE WORLD OF FREEDOM AND DEMOCRACY UNDER GOD'S TRUTH

Paperback • 312 pages • $15.95
ISBN: 978-1-942125-60-0

This is a compilation of select international lectures given by Ryuho Okawa during his (ongoing) global missionary tours. It espouses that freedom and democracy are vital principles to foster peace and shared prosperity, if adopted universally.

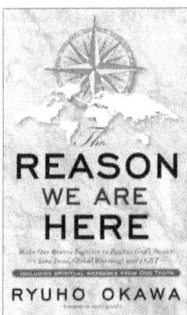

THE REASON WE ARE HERE
MAKE OUR POWERS TOGETHER TO REALIZE GOD'S JUSTICE -CHINA ISSUE, GLOBAL WARMING, AND LGBT-

Paperback • 215 pages • $14.95
ISBN: 978-1-943869-62-6

The Reason We Are Here is a book of thought that is unlike any other: its global perspective, timely opinion on current issues, and spiritual class are unmatched. The main content is the lecture in Toronto, Canada given in October 2019 by Ryuho Okawa, a Japanese spiritual leader and the national teacher of Japan.

For a complete list of books, visit okawabooks.com

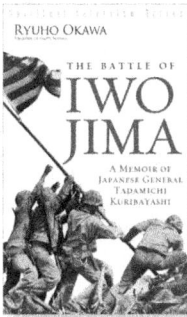

THE BATTLE OF IWO JIMA

A MEMOIR OF JAPANESE GENERAL TADAMICHI KURIBAYASHI

Paperback • 174 pages • $9.95
ISBN: 978-1-941779-89-7

"I believe that offering *The Battle of Iwo Jima: A Memoir of Japanese General Tadamichi Kuribayashi* to the world will finally draw a line, 70 years after the end of WWII... I believe Japan and the U.S. should not have been enemies, but instead friends."
                                                    -From Afterword

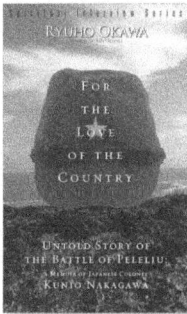

FOR THE LOVE OF THE COUNTRY

UNTOLD STORY OF THE BATTLE OF PELELIU: A MEMOIR OF JAPANESE COLONEL KUNIO NAKAGAWA

Paperback • 159 pages • $9.95
ISBN: 978-1-941779-62-0

"If the most intense decisive battle between Japan and the U.S. on Peleliu Island had been covered accurately and impartially by the U.S. media during WWII... we can speculate that the Korean War, the Vietnam War and even the Iraq War may not have happened."   -From Preface

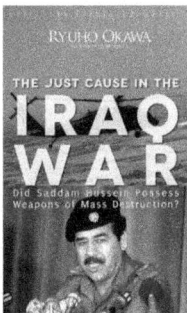

THE JUST CAUSE IN THE IRAQ WAR

DID SADDAM HUSSEIN POSSESS WEAPONS OF MASS DESTRUCTION?

Paperback • 223 pages • $14.95
ISBN: 978-1-937673-41-3

In this book, you will discover that Saddam Hussein was also behind the planning of the 9/11 terrorist attacks and both he and Osama bin Laden are now in Hell. The knowledge this book provides will help each of us make the right decisions as we work together to create a peaceful international society.

For a complete list of books, visit okawabooks.com

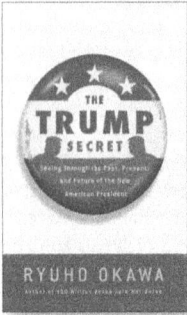

THE TRUMP SECRET

Seeing Through the Past, Present, and Future of the New American President

Paperback • 208 pages • $14.95
ISBN: 978-1-942125-22-8

This book contains a series of lectures and interviews that unveil the secrets to Trump's victory and makes predictions of what will happen under his presidency. This book predicts the coming of a new America that will go through a great transformation from the "red and blue states" to the United States.

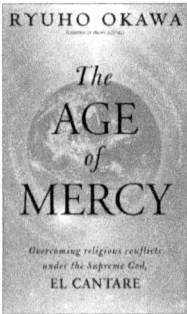

THE AGE OF MERCY

Overcoming religious conflicts under the Supreme God, El Cantare

Hardcover • 110 pages • $22.95
ISBN: 978-1-943869-51-0

Why are there conflicts in the world? How can people understand each other better? This book is a message from the Supreme God who has been guiding humankind from the beginning of creation.

INTO THE STORM OF INTERNATIONAL POLITICS
THE NEW STANDARDS OF THE WORLD ORDER

Paperback • 154 pages • $14.95
ISBN:978-1-941779-27-9

The world is now seeking a new idea or a new philosophy that will show the countries with such values the direction they should head in. In this book, Okawa presents new standards of the world order while giving his own analysis on world affairs concerning the U.S., China, Islamic State and others.

For a complete list of books, visit okawabooks.com

THE ROYAL ROAD OF LIFE
Beginning Your Path of Inner Peace, Virtue, and a Life of Purpose

THE LAWS OF GREAT ENLIGHTENMENT
Always Walk with Buddha

I CAN
Discover Your Power Within

HONG KONG REVOLUTION
Spiritual Messages of the Guardian Spirits of Xi Jinping and
Agnes Chow Ting

SPIRITUAL MESSAGES FROM OSCAR WILDE
Love, Beauty, and LGBT

THE STARTING POINT OF HAPPINESS
An Inspiring Guide to Positive Living with Faith, Love, and
Courage

HEALING FROM WITHIN
Life-Changing Keys to Calm, Spiritual, and Healthy Living

THE UNHAPPINESS SYNDROME
28 Habits of Unhappy People (and How to Change Them)

THINK BIG!
Be Positive and Be Brave to Achieve Your Dreams

For a complete list of books, visit okawabooks.com

MUSIC BY RYUHO OKAWA

El Cantare Ryuho Okawa Original Songs

A song celebrating Lord God

A song celebrating Lord God,
the God of the Earth,
who is beyond a prophet.

DVD
CD

The Water Revolution

English and Chinese version

For the truth and happiness of the 1.4 billion people in China who have no freedom. Love, justice, and sacred rage of God are on this melody that will give you courage to fight to bring peace.

DVD

CD

Search on YouTube

the water revolution 🔍 for a short ad!

Listen now today!

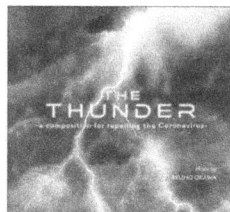

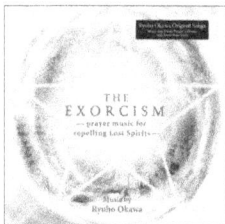

165

www.ingramcontent.com/pod-product-compliance
Lightning Source LLC
Chambersburg PA
CBHW032058020426
42335CB00011B/391